Christmas 1997

Paul – This is highly
recommended reading for your
"stage" in life.

GEMS
OF
CHINESE WISDOM

智
囊

Much love these
many years!

Eleanor
Bill and Mr.
PSBDG

ASIAPAC COMIC SERIES
STRATEGY & LEADERSHIP

Mastering the Art of Leadership

GEMS
OF
CHINESE WISDOM

智囊

WANG XUANMING

Translated by
Leong Weng Kam

ASIAPAC • SINGAPORE

Publisher
ASIAPAC BOOKS PTE LTD
629 Aljunied Road #04-06
Cititech Industrial Building
Singapore 1438
Tel: 7453868
Fax: 7453822

First published September 1993

© ASIAPAC BOOKS, 1993
ISBN 981-3029-08-0

Cover design by Bay Song Lin
Typeset by Unistar Graphics Pte Ltd
Body text in 8/9 pt Helvetica
Printed in Singapore by
Loi Printing Pte Ltd

Publisher's Note

Comics play an important role in our fast-moving urban society. They serve the young as well as the adult readers. Comics are fun and entertaining. They can also be a kind of satire and can even make classical literature and philosophy available to us in a light-hearted way.

We are pleased to present the work of Wang Xuanming, a contemporary cartoonist from Mainland China, who has illustrated a series of ancient Chinese military classics into comics. The first two books, *Thirty-six Stratagems* and *Six Strategies for War* have been warmly received by our readers. *Gems of Chinese Wisdom* is the third book in this series.

We feel honoured to have the cartoonist Wang Xuanming's permission to the translation rights to his best-selling comics. We would also like to thank Mr Leong Weng Kam for translating this volume and writing the Introduction, Mr Chiang Ming Yu for his review, and the production team for putting in their best effort in the publication of this series.

Titles in the Strategy and Leadership series:

Like a jar of good wine, *Gems of Chinese Wisdom* is difficult to put down until, all too soon, it has been finished. But unlike wine, *Gems of Chinese Wisdom* can be enjoyed again and again, until its lessons become familiar.

Gems of Chinese Wisdom may seem to be didactic at times, but the reader has to remember that when the book *Zhinang*, from which it has been adapted from, was first written, China was going through troubled times. Feng Menglong wrote *Zhinang* in the hope that someone would be inspired by it and save China from ruin.

More than 350 years later, we are able to enjoy Feng Menglong's work without the immediate attendant troubles of the times which Feng Menglong faced. However, the same problems of the Ming Dynasty's twilight years can still be found in other parts of the world, and we would do well to learn what lessons of wisdom there are to be found before these problems come to us.

It is a pity that not all of *Zhinang* could be included in *Gems of Chinese Wisdom*, which presents only a portion of the original work. Still, artist Wang Xuanming deserves the highest praise for doing so much to make wisdom accessible, not only through the publication of *Gems of Chinese Wisdom*, but also through the publication of translations of two of his other books; *Thirty-Six Stratagems* and *Six Strategies for War*. More books are yet to come and I wish the translators all speed in their work! For now, I wish the readers many happy hours of reading and learning.

Chiang Ming Yu
Chairman, Wargame Club
Singapore Armed Forces Reservists' Association

About the Editor/Illustrator

Wang Xuanming, a contemporary cartoonist in China, was born in Beijing in 1950. He was trained formally in commercial art and industrial art. Since 1972, he has been engaged in various aspects of artistic work, even undertaking the production of screen advertisements and artistic stage designs. Wang's contribution to the field of art is immense. He frequently explores various ways of expressing his artistic talents. Besides a lot of cartoons, picture books, and illustrations, he also does oil paintings and posters. His works have on many occasions entered nationwide art exhibitions, won awards in several art competitions, and have been selected for inclusion in various art albums.

Wang's cartoons, illustrations, and other works have been serialized in all the major newspapers and publications in Beijing since 1980. His cartoons entitled *Different Gravitational Force* is praised by famous Chinese artists, and was selected for inclusion in the *Anthology of Chinese Scientific Cartoons*. In 1987, he participated in the creation of the animated cartoon *Brother Elephant*, which captured the hearts of many children when it was first shown on television.

Wang has worked with many publishers in Beijing, such as China Friendly Publishing Co., Chinese Cultural Publishing Co., Huaxia Publishing Co., People's Art Publishing Co., and Zhaohua Publishing Co. He has gained the trust and confidence of both publishers and artists alike.

In his latest comic series, *Books of Strategy*, he uses a simple and humorous art form to introduce ancient Chinese military classics to modern readers. The books were very well received by people from all walks of life when they were first published in China; the Beijing Radio Station made a special interview of this series of books and highly recommended it to the public. This series is published by China Friendly Publishing Co. in China, and by Treasure Creation Co. Ltd. in Hongkong. Asiapac Books in Singapore is the publisher for the English edition of this series.

Wang is at present an art editor at the *China Science and Technology Daily*.

Introduction

Only fools do not learn from the mistakes in life. Sometimes, we may even need to pay a high price for a lesson or two about life's painful and yet simple truths. But what perhaps separates us from the truly wise is the fact that they are able to learn from the experiences and mistakes of others while we continue to draw lessons only from our own follies. One simple way to wise up at the expense of others, therefore, is to learn from the things said and done by the men and women who lived before us. Even the sage, Confucius, had this to say: "Gain new insights by studying the past!"

There is much to learn from the Chinese civilization with its long history in which fascinating stories of people who won the day by showing remarkable wit and sorrowful tales of others who failed as they succumbed to their weaknesses abound. These include stories of princes who gained the throne by outwitting their rivals and tales of housewives whose wisdom helped motivate husbands to work hard and keep their mothers-in-law happy at the same time. They provide valuable lessons in life for readers throughout the ages.

Zhinang (*Gems of Chinese Wisdom*) is a collection of these ancient tales and amusing anecdotes which occured over a period of more than 3,500 years in Chinese history, from the first Chinese empire, Xia, to the later part of the Ming Dynasty. It is the work of the famous Ming scholar, Feng Menglong, who was said to have written this classic of nearly 300,000 words in just two months nearly 400 years ago. The stories were culled from history books, classical literature, official and unofficial documents as well as popular legends.

Besides giving the reader a glimpse of Chinese history, the stories as they are retold in the book, show both the wisdom and folly of the Chinese who lived -- from kings to the commoners -- in the way they governed the state, the strategies they used in politics and warfare, the reasoning behind judicial decisions, the principles involved in the conduct of businesses and relationships. The stories, which had been passed down from generation to generation before they were compiled in book form by Feng Menglong, were so well-liked and unforgettable that some of them even became the sources from which

Chinese proverbs and sayings had their origins. The book, it was learned, was among the few "must read" Chinese literary works on the late Chinese leader, Chairman Mao Zedong's reading list.

Wisdom is necessary for success. This is true for the politician, the military commander as well as the businessman. It is also for the ordinary man or woman who seeks only the simple goals in life. For those who already know, wisdom is wisdom no matter where it is used. Once a person has it, he or she will be successful in any situation.

Cartoonist Wang Xuanming's version of Feng Menglong's masterpiece is an excellent book for modern-day readers who find the original work in classical Chinese archaic and perhaps even difficult to comprehend. From some 1,000 stories in the original text, the comic version has condensed and summarised them to around 100, making reading much easier. They are divided into 10 chapters as in the original in prose, with each describing a particular aspect of wisdom.

The comic version in modern Chinese, first published three years ago in China and later in Hong Kong, is a best-seller today. It brings to the attention of modern-day readers a classic almost forgotten. I hope the English translation of this version can do the same and benefit those who will otherwise miss the gems of Chinese wisdom from a civilization more than 5,000 years old.

Leong Weng Kam

Leong Weng Kam is presently a bilingual journalist with The Straits Times of Singapore.

Feng Menglong

Feng Menglong (1574-1646), a
native of Changzhou (now Jiangsu
province), was a literary giant in
his time. His masterpiece, *Zhinang*,
the book of wisdom, was written in
1626.

Feng Menglong

Feng Menglong lived during the last days of the Ming Dynasty when there was war almost all year round. He hoped someone wise would come forward to save the country from ruin.

1

He had a hard life and he understood society ills and corruption in the courts well. He finished writing *Zhinang* within two months. The book was based on the wisdom of great men in Chinese history. He hoped his fellow countrymen could learn from them.

2

Feng Menglong said:
Man needs wisdom as much as land needs water. If there is no water in the ground, the land will be charred. A man without wisdom is like a walking corpse.

3

Water fills both the low and hollow areas. Therefore, it is easier for man to become wise in times of difficulties.

WISDOM

4

5

Man's inborn wisdom is like water hidden under the rocks. It will never surface.

True learning means discovering the water and allowing it to flow. Let my book be like the shovel to unearth man's wisdom.

6

**Supreme
Wisdom**

1. Wisdom is fluid like. Its usefulness lies in the right application. An intelligent person may fail because he considered too many things while a stupid person may sometimes succeed by acting correctly only once.

2. Why?

   That's because true wisdom doesn't come from our thoughts alone. It is based on feelings and facts.

3. Most people are concerned with only short-term gains. The truly wise look at the future.

4. Most people fret when things go wrong. The truly wise remain calm and handle the situation with ease.

5. No matter what difficulties they face, the truly wise will still press on . . .

6. They calculate while appearing inactive and are able to win even from afar. Their actions are often within reason, unexpected and unchallengeable.

   I'm really impressed. Supreme Wisdom indeed!

7

9

6 I wish to follow the example of a would-be emperor. But I've nobody worthy to call my teacher!

7 Sir, if you wish to build up the state and attract talent, you can start with me, your loyal servant, Guo Hui.

8 So King Zhao built a beautiful residence for Guo Hui and accorded him with the respect of a teacher.

9 Within the next three years, other able men such as Su Qin, Zou Yan, Yue Yi and Qu Jing were also attracted to serve in the state of Yan.

10

Guo Hui's ability to attract many talented people lived up to his reputation as a wise official and teacher.

11

Although Yong Chi was not well liked by the Han Emperor, Gao Zu, he was still made a member of the nobility for his war achievements.

12

After defeating Liu Zhang, Liu Bei still treated Xu Jing, the senior strategist of the kingdom of Shu with respect. His action earned him the loyalty from every soldier and official.

When recruiting, always pay respect to talent. That is the way to make a country strong and its citizens prosperous. Only the foolish do otherwise.

Magnanimity

1

While the Northern Song general, Guo Jin, was making his rounds in Shanxi, an army colonel filed a complaint against him to the emperor.

Guo Jin is guilty of this, that and the other . . .

2

When the emperor discovered that the complaints were false, he sent him back to Shanxi and ordered Guo Jin to execute him.

3

Guo Jin told the colonel:

How dare you make those false accusations? I admire your guts.

Courage to admit our faults

1

When Xu Cunzhai was an examiner, he gave a D grade for a student's essay because he thought some parts of the script were plagiarized from a famous writer's works.

This deserves only a D!

2

I was only quoting his work in my essay. I never said it was written by me.

The student brought the original work to him and explained:

3

Oh, it's my mistake.

15

5 How do you get honour?

6 You only owned Xue Di, the country, not its people whom you showed no love for. You are only thinking of ways to exploit them.

On your behalf, I have ordered the people there to burn away all their IOU's. They were very happy and shouted in praise of you. This is "honour" I've got for you.

7

8 You have lost my money and still think you are clever?

9 A year later, the king of Qi removed Meng Changjun from his post and allowed him to return to Xue Di. Before his arrival, he saw people there lining up to welcome him from miles away.

Honour is indeed precious.

Welcome!

Although the earthly treasures are precious, their worth can be calculated. But honour, on the other hand, is priceless. Those who can recognise this will be able to do great things for the country.

17

Foresight

遠猶卷

Avoid strategies that lack foresight. Man's social status and fortunes changes constantly. When a mature person predicts life's changes, he should look at the long-term rather than the short-term to avoid mistakes.

Losing power for a few drinks

1
After gaining power, Song Emperor, Tai Zu, asked his counsel, Zhao Pu:

For decades since the last day of the Tang Dynasty, there were many changes of rulers and much fighting over the throne. Why?

2
That was because the officials' power became too strong and the emperor's weak. Only by reducing their power and influence in the military, can there be peace.

3
Soon Emperor Tai Zu invited Shi Shouxin and two of his other top military commanders to dinner.

19

No news is good news.

1　Chen Shu was in charge of the treasury during the rule of Song Emperor, Zhen Zhong.

2　The emperor ordered him:

Tell me what we have in our reserves.

Yes sir.

After a long period of time.

Where is the report?

3

4　The emperor ordered his Prime Minister to ask Chen Shu for an explanation.

Why didn't you report to the emperor?

The emperor is too young. If he knows there is so much in the treasury, he is likely to become a spendthrift.

One must prevent oneself from complacency and not think only of enjoying life especially when the going is good.

5 Using a special mail as a means of communication can become a habit and that's bad in the long run.

6 What if an ambitious official use it to prevent links between the court and the people? The consequences can be disastrous.

7 After listening, Emperor Xiao Zhong was full of praises for him:

Very good. You're very thorough in your analysis.

I refuse to accept the special power you give me because of the harm it can bring.

Special powers go beyond the laws of the state and they are harmful to both the country and its people. Only the truly wise can see the potential problems they can create.

Criticisms

Opinions

Petitions

Don't do for the name's sake.

Li You, the newly promoted army chief of the Tang Dynasty attracted many would-be relatives.

Let's see.

Will your daughter marry my son?

1

2
One day, Li called all his colleagues together.

3
I'm hopeful because I'm powerful.

My family is famous.

Luck is with me.

Hee! Hee!

I'm choosing my son-in-law.

4
But Li chosed a young and the most junior officer instead.

I know you're not married. Please take my daughter's hand.

!?

I've seen too many court officials unite with the rich and famous families by marriage. But most of their children are so useless. One must always depend on one's own abilities.

23

Simplicity

通簡卷

Most things in life are the works of the mediocre. One can easily deal with matters using understanding. It's as simple as using sunlight to melt ice.

I'm drunk too.

Two officials quarreled over their contributions to the Song Emperor, Tai Zhong.

2 Someone advised the emperor:

Forget it.

They failed to observe etiquette. Punish them.

3 The next day, they recovered from their drunkness and apologized to the emperor.

4 Emperor Tai Zhong said:

I couldn't remember. I was drunk too.

In this way, respect for the court is maintained and the drunkards were also taught a lesson.

The wise acting foolish

Staying cool in a crisis

1. The Northern Song general, Li Yunze, was hosting a banquet in the camp when the armoury suddenly caught fire.

2. Unperturbed, Li Yunze continued to wine and dine.

3. The fire was put out in a short while.

4. Meanwhile, Li Yunze sent someone quietly to Yingzhou.

5. Within 10 days the weapons packed in tea boxes arrived from Yingzhou. The weapons destroyed in the fire were replaced secretly.

6. But someone complained against Li Yunze before Emperor Zhen Zhong. Ask him why.

He's guilty. He didn't stop the banquet to put out the fire.

Fire safety precautions in the armoury are army secrets. We were dining when fire broke out. I suspect it was the job of an internal spy. We would fall into his trap if we rush to put out the fire.

Not moved by changes

1 During the period of the Three Kingdoms, General Zhang Liao was asked to lead a big army to Chang She.

2 There were rebels in the army.

3 A fire broke out in the middle of the night and the entire army was in chaos.

4 Zhang Liao told his men:

Don't move! Someone is trying to create trouble.

5 Zhang Liao and his loyal soldiers stayed motionless in the camp.

Keep still if you are not a rebel.

The culprits were spotted almost immediately. It's a virtue to stay calm even when things go wrong.

28

An open-chested policy

1. The doors to the house of Tang Dynasty senior official, Guo Ziyi, are always open to visitors.

2. One day, an officer who was going away on assignment came to bid him goodbye.

3. The officer was surprised to see Guo Ziyi running around like a servant in the house, helping his daughter to wash up.

   "Get me some water."

   "Coming."

4. His sons cried, begging him to change his ways.

   "Father, you're a highly respected figure. You shouldn't allow anyone to walk freely into your house."

5. "You don't know my intentions. All that I owned came from the generosity of the court."

6 If I kept my walls high and shut my doors, I'll not live to regret when someone bad mouthed me or say I'm disloyal to the ruler out of jealousy. My family may face execution as a result of their smear campaign.

7 Now, I'm as open as a book. Anyone can see me clearly from inside and outside.

8 Even if someone wanted to slander me, he cannot succeed because the truth is known by everybody.

The best defence against slanders is the truth. The open-chested person is never afraid to tell all to the world.

Courage

迎刃卷

The mediocre will be helpless in a crisis whereby the cliff blocks the roads ahead and the rough sea seals off the retreat route. Only the truly wise and brilliant who are in control can find a way out by the use of strategies. They do so with ease, like an excellent cook butchering a cow.

The soft option

1 During the reign of Tang Emperor, De Zhong, the military strategist, Wang Jiahe was powerful because the army was under his control.

2 If I replaced him, he might just stage a military coup.

Emperor De Zhong was very troubled.

3 Emperor De Zhong consulted his Prime Minister Cui Youbu.

How do I deal with Wang Jiahe?

I've a solution.

4. Cui Youbu invited Wang Jiahe to his house for "talks".

5. Cui Youbu deliberately allowed their discussion to drag.

With due respect to you, I like to make five proposals . . .

6.

Forty . . .

7. While they were having their discussion, Bai Zizhen arrived at the army to take over Wang Jiahe's post as commander of the troops.

If my opponent had tried to remove me by force, they wouldn't succeed because power was in my hands. But I was caught off-guard as they had cheated me in a quiet scheme.

The art of moderation

1 During the reign of Song Emperor, Zhen Zhong, the Mongolian state of Qi Tan asked for a loan in addition to the annual gifts the Song Dynasty had promised.

The situation along the eastern border is very tense and the state of Qi Tan is preparing to attack us.

2 Emperor Zhen Zhong consulted his Prime Minister Wang Dan.

To loan or not to loan?

3 Qi Tan is using the loan to test our reaction. We must agree to give them the $30,000 loan. Tell them, repayments will be deducted from our gifts next year.

4 The state of Qi Tan felt ashamed after receiving the loan.

Forget about the repayments from the state of Qi Tan. Continue to send them our gifts.

The next year, Wang Dan gave this order to his official:

5

34

Isolating the culprit

Jiang Pin is in control of a large army. His aides are also veterans in war.

Ming Emperor, Wu Zhong, was seriously ill. His senior official Yang Shizhai wanted to capture the general Jiang Pin.

2 To nab him rashly may force him to stage a military coup.

3 General Wang Jinxi offered a plan:

Try sending Jiang Pin's forces to Tongzhou in the name of registering and honouring their contributions.

4 Unaware of the scheme, Jiang Pin sent his men to receive their honour in Tongzhou.

Yang Shizhai caught Jiang Pin easily this way. Narrowing one's target by isolating the culprit is an effective means to defeat one's enemy.

Wisdom in Understanding

BRIGHT

Since the beginning of the Universe, all things can be separated by these two words, "brightness" and "darkness".

1

2

DARK

There is darkness when Heaven and Earth are closed. There is light only when they open up.

3 A country will be thrown into darkness when its rulers are unsure of themselves.

Unclean water will give a stench, metal not polished will go rusty and thoughts unclear will put man in a hazy state.

The sly will choose the dark and narrow way, the noble will take the bright and open path.

4

5

6 Those who cannot think are like walking with a small candle in darkness where vision is limited.

7 The stupid are like the blind riding a blind horse. They cannot help falling into the depths of the valleys.

8

Thus, there are great differences in the thoughts of man. While the dull are still puzzled, the bright ones already found the solutions.

The intelligent can uncover mysteries, solve problems and avoid tragedies. They can also benefit from their experiences to achieve success.

Intelligence is something we always need.

9

知微卷

Details

Failure or a dead end are situations which the wise will never get themselves into. They are able to spot a problem even before it appears, nipping it in the bud with a ready solution.

The root of the problem

1 King Zhou ordered his craftsmen to make him a pair of ivory chopsticks. His advisor, Ji Zi, was very worried with what he saw.

2 Ivory chopsticks need to be matched by jade wine cups, and rare delicacies on the table . . .

Ji Zi said:

3 And a luxurious lifestyle of greed.

In the end King Zhou was killed in the fury of a popular uprising.

The importance of rewards

1 Zi Gong, a native of Lu state, found a long-lost fellow countryman in a neighboring state.

2 Going by our laws, this is your reward.

I don't want it.

3 Confucius said: Rewards are given to encourage good work. If you refuse to accept them, who will do good in future?

4 Zi Lu saved a man from drowning.

5 The man gave him a buffalo to thank him. Zi Lu accepted the good gesture.

From now on, there will be many who will come forward to do good.

A good judge of man

42

11 King Huan Gong dismissed the four after Guan Zhong's death.

But three years later, King Huan Gong invited them back to the court.

I think Guan Zhong has been too harsh on them.

12

13 The next year, Chang Zhiwu created a rumour out of King Huan Gong's illness.

The king will die on such and such a day.

14 Hunger. Hunger. Hunger. Hunger.

The four men took the opportunity to create trouble by imprisoning the king.

Guan Zhong was a good judge of man. He was able to see further into a problem.

43

The need for compassion

1 Zhang Zhongding returned home from work.

Who dares to sleep in my living room?

2 Zhang asked him:

Anything happened in your family?

Yes, my mother has been ill for a long time. My brother is not back from his trip.

3 Zhang Zhongding sent someone investigate.

It's true.

4 A person was hired immediately to look after his mother.

5 He slept in my living room because his worries have affected his moods.

If a master can show such compassion, no one will refuse to serve him.

44

臆中卷

Conjecture

To be able to assess and predict the outcome of an event, it is necessary to know the facts and its sources. One cannot be fooled by schemes of any kind with such knowledge.

Know your opponent

1 Fan Sui and Wang Ji left the state of Wei secretly for the state of Qin. They saw a horse carriage coming after them.

I heard Lang Hou is a very mean fellow. I'm afraid he'll humiliate me. I better hide myself inside the carriage.

It's the Prime Minister making his rounds.

Fan Sui knew the Qin's Prime Minister, Lang Hou, too well. He said:

2

The perils of public hatred

1. The king of Qin asked his adviser, Shi Yang:

Tell me, who among the officials in the state of Jin will be destroyed first?

The Luan family.

2. Luan Ya is corrupt and his son, Luan Yin, will be the unlucky one.

3. Luan Wuzi treated the people so well that they even worshipped the tree outside his house. That helped to ensure the safety of his son, Luan Ya.

4. Luan Ya survived because of his father's good deeds. But in Luan Yin's generation, the family sowed only hatred, not gratitude, among the people.

Even the fate of a country lies in the hearts of its people. What more a family?

Seize the opportunity

1. Many questions were raised when Cao Cao decided to attack Liu Bei from the east.

Yuan Shao will ambush us from behind.

If we lose our retreat route, we can neither attack nor defend.

2.

3. Cao Cao said:

Liu Bei has only begun to establish his foothold. We'll win in a swift attack. This is too good an opportunity to miss. Attack right away!

Yuan Shao is far too cautious. I don't think he'll act fast enough to send his troops against us.

49

The art of negotiation

1 The Qin general Wang Qi attacked the state of Zhao, causing it to suffer successive defeats.

2 The king of Zhao wanted to negotiate for peace. But his adviser, Lu Qing said:

Qin's objective is to defeat Zhao's army. As they're taking the initiative, I don't think they want peace.

3 We can try to bribe both the states of Chu and Wei. When the Qins think that we are combining our forces, the chance of a negotiation for peace will be good.

4 But the king of Zhao still want to seek peace first.

Zheng Zhu, I'm sending you to seek peace.

5 Lu Qing again advised the king of Zhao:

The state of Qin will tell the world that you're begging for peace. And when other states refuse to rush to your aid, it'll be impossible for you to seek peace.

The result was as Lu Qing had expected. Creating suspicion in negotiations is still the most effective.

剖疑卷

Analysis

Rumours can create havoc. In a world full of wickedness and the callousness with which people are made to suffer, how can one progress and move forward if one's vision is blurred? Let's hope wisdom is like the sun, capable of destroying all evil.

51

Unperturbed by chaos

It rained 40 days and 40 nights during the early years of the Han Emperor, Cheng Di's reign. There were chaos in the capital.

Floods coming!

Escape!

Escape!

1

2

General Wang Feng said:

Emperor, get onto the boat. The others get up to the city walls.

The army's second-in-command, general Wang Shang said:

From time immemorial, there wasn't a time when the capital was flooded. They must be rumours.

3

5 Later, investigations confirmed that they were truly rumours.

Rumours.

Commanding the people to go up the city wall can create even more chaos.

4

To make the right decision, remain calm always.

Fight poison with poison

1. During the rule of Wei Wenhou, people were complaining to the newly appointed governor of the Ye county, Ximen Bao:

Our miseries were caused by the need of the river god to have a new wife each year.

2. The county officials were in collaboration with witches. They made money by holding an elaborate wedding ceremony for the river god each year. The witches would force pretty girls to become the river god's concubines.

Marry her off.

3. Many girls were drowned in the "marriage", forcing parents to run away with their daughters. Soon, the county became a deserted city.

Help!

4. I'll send off the girl myself when the river god wants to wed again.

54

Choice

經務卷

In the eyes of the needy, even an ordinary looking gourd is precious because it can help to save lives. Though it may not be of the best material, lead can still be used to make weapons such as swords. It is better than making leaves out of ivory because they are only good as ornaments. The wise are therefore those who know the time and situation well.

On fair punishment

1 The nobility had, during the period of the Song Dynasty, cultivated their own crops by opening up government dykes.

Zhao Changyan, an official from Zhizhou, did not take any action.   2

I know.

That's how they did it.

3 The dykes burst again.

One day...

4 Quick, use the grass from the homes of the noble to block them up!

Since then, nobody dare open up the government dykes anymore. To punish the arrogant at the right moment is the most effective way to teach them a lesson.

Turning harm into something good

After the Song Dynasty official Zhao Kai implemented the use of paper currency, the citizens found shopping more convenient.

1

2

One day, a group of men were caught making counterfeit notes.

3 Prime Minister Zhang Jun and Zhao Kai discussed ways to punish the culprits.

They should be given the death sentence!

I don't think it's a good idea.

After adding the seal of the state's treasurer to these counterfeit notes, they will become real money as well.

4

And allow the culprits to continue manufacturing money after charging them.

5

This is what every able government administrator should learn to do. To turn a harmful event into something good for the people through simple administrative means.

Zhao Kai said:

Finding the root of the problem

1 It was during the Song Dynasty when a famine broke out. The price of rice rocketed, resulting in many people starving to death.

2 Notices were put up in every province and district warning rice merchants against increasing prices further.

Notice

No Price Hike

But the ration official representing both the Yue and Zhi provinces said:

Yes!

Put up new notices, lift control over the prices.

3

4 Rice merchants everywhere rushed to sell their stocks in Yuezhou and prices plummeted instead.

Always go to the root of the problem when seeking for the solution. Those who treat only the head for headache, look only at the feet when the limbs are painful will go a long way before finding the cure.

Wisdom in Observation

1

The truly wise pay great attention to night patrol, carrying out investigation in areas unknown to others. They hope to discover more secrets by doing so.

2

Isn't it good to have eyes as bright and sharp as Shun Di's to examine matters clearly?

As the saying goes, one's ability to see the fish even in deep sea spells a bad omen.

3

Without good eyesight, one can fall down easily in the dark.

4

One cannot hope to investigate without vision. And if there is no investigation, there is no way you can show your understanding.

Exploit one's weakness

Solving the case with borrowed pigs

1. My sister-in-law set the house on fire and my brother was burned alive. Give me justice.

During the period of the Three Kingdoms, magistrate Zhang Ju of the state of Wu, was hearing a case:

2. Zhang Ju ordered: Give me a live pig and a dead one.

3. Burn the two pigs in a fire.

4. After the fire was put out, the mouth of the live pig was filled with ashes.

5. But inside the mouth of the original dead pig, there were no ashes.

Examine the dead man's mouth to see if there were ashes in it and that determined whether he was killed before or after the fire.

65

Gold turned into stones

1 A farmer who lived in Shanxi during the Tang Dynasty dug up an earthern jar filled with gold ingots. The gold was certified by provincial officials.

2 To play safe, the provincial governor had the gold ingots carried to his home for keeping.

Funny, the gold have turned into stones?!!

Two nights later, the governor went to look at them. 3

5 Yuan Zi was asked to hear the case.

This big jar can contain 250 gold ingots.

4 The governor couldn't explain and was charged.

Act swiftly on complex matters.

68

Rats' faeces in honey

Evil

詰奸卷

If the legal system is unjust and when laws are not strictly enforced, court officials will be complacent and evil doings will abound. One should treat the evil doers like farmers do with pests; kill them instantly with insecticide.

Divide and destroy

When the Ming Dynasty general Qian Zao was stationed in Mi Yun, two of his men committed armed robbery.

1

The local official charged them in court but they plead not guilty.

2

3

The official sought General Qian Zao's help.

The two soldiers are tough. I don't know what to do with them.

71

The heart of the matter

When the Song official Liu Zai was the governor of Taizhou, someone filed a suit before him.

1
I lost a gold hair pin

2
There were only two maids in the house.

Who stole it?

Not me.

I don't know.

Liu Zai gave them a piece of reed each.

3
If you are not guilty, the reed will not change tomorrow. If you're, it will grow by two inches.

4
The next day, one of the maid's reed was shorter by two inches.

5
How can the reed grow? It's your guilty conscience at work. You cut it shorter.

I'm guilty.

The guilty are never on firm ground. When they try to conceal their guilt, they'll inevitably show themselves up.

Spotting an adultery by taking heed to details

1 During the Song Dynasty, two men fought after some heavy drinking.

2 After the first man returned home, he was killed in his sleep when both his feet were chopped off.

3 You killed my husband!

His wife filed a suit against the second man.

4 The district judge Yuan Jiang told the dead man's wife:

The accused has pleaded guilty. You may go back to prepare the funeral.

Beyond common sense

75

The fall of the greedy

1 During the period of the Five Dynasties, a Later Han official at Taining, Murong Yanchao, started a pawn shop.

Hee! Hee! I'm rich.

2 A wicked fellow brought two pieces of faked silver to the shop one day.

3 They were discovered only later.

It's all iron inside the silver.

4 Murong Yanchao devised a plan:

Tonight, open a hole at the back of the shop and move all the valuables to another place.

The shop is burgled!

6 Murong Yanchao also announced the theft in public.

Report your pawned items and we'll compensate you accordingly.

5

Wisdom in Decision

1 Those capable of taking on the responsibility of the state need to have courage. And those who succeed in the task must be men with exceptional intelligence and strategies.

2 Man can be drowned in water.

And be burned to death by fire. **3**

To stay away from water and fire knowing that they have no mercy is wisdom, not cowardice. But do not fear them if one can control the two elements.

4

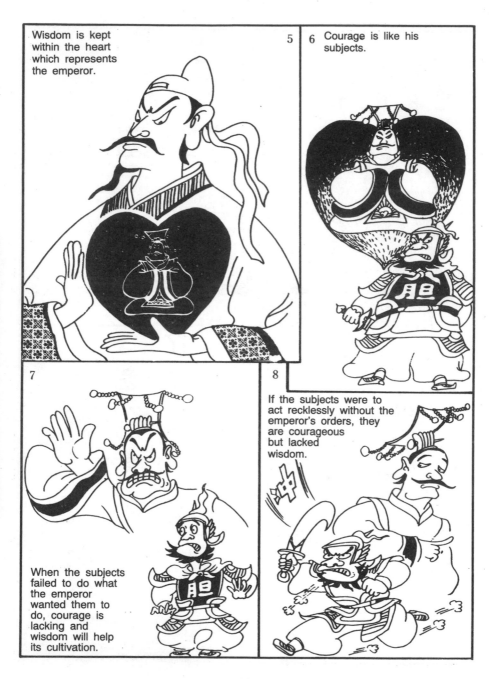

5 Wisdom is kept within the heart which represents the emperor.

6 Courage is like his subjects.

7 When the subjects failed to do what the emperor wanted them to do, courage is lacking and wisdom will help its cultivation.

8 If the subjects were to act recklessly without the emperor's orders, they are courageous but lacked wisdom.

9 胆

Wisdom gives rise to courage, not the other way. Wisdom can contain recklessness and it is also courage's guiding post.

10 Zhao Siguan from the period of Five Dynasties believed that he would become more courageous by swallowing other people's gall-bladders. But it only showed his stupidity.

11 To learn from the wise and improve on one's wisdom is the best way to build up courage. The wiser person, the more courageous the person will become.

Suppression

威克卷

One who dares step on the tiger's tail will not be bitten by the tiger. One who dares whip the dragon, will get the pearl from its mouth. Are both the tiger and dragon fools? No, it is all because of man's superior wisdom.

A man of great courage

1

During the Eastern Han period, General Ban Chao led a group of his men for a visit to the neighbouring state of Shan Shan in the west. They were warmly greeted by its king.

2

But later, the king of Shan Shan turned cold towards Ban Chao, keeping his distance.

3

It must be the arrival of the diplomats from the Xiongnu state. The king is undecided which state to pledge his allegience.

84

Conceal the motive to kill

1. Han Emperor, Wu Di, told his official, Geng Chun:

According to reliable sources, the governor of Zhending is planning a coup to overthrow me. Arrest him now!

2. Geng Chun pretended he was making a courtesy call when he arrived at Zhending.

3. Liu Yang didn't go out to welcome Geng Chun by saying he was ill. He invited Geng to his residence in a letter instead.

You're invited.

4. Geng Chun replied to the letter. Liu Yang read:

I'm on an emperor's mission. You should come to meet me even though you are ill.

The art of punishment

8 Kuang Zhong ordered his guards to throw them high into the air where they fell and died. After the killings the others never dared do wrong again.

9 One day, the carelessness of a junior officer led to a fire and many important documents were destroyed.

10 Give him a beating and send him home.

Kuang Zhong shouted at the officer.

11 Kuang Zhong wrote to the emperor, admitting full responsibility for the fire.

12 It's my responsibility. How can I allow a junior officer to bear it?

Why didn't you give him the death sentence?

A good law enforcer sees no distinction between the senior and junior officers when meeting out punishment. However, he must know when to be strict, when to be lenient.

Timing

識斷卷

Wisdom results in understanding which in turn offers solutions. When a decision is not forthcoming at the opportune time, disaster may follow.

The rule of law

1 A prisoner from the state of Wei escaped to a neighbouring state.

2

No.

The king of Wei sent his official to the state.

My king will give you gold in exchange for the culprit.

Use gentleness to subjugate hardness

1. It was during the rule of Ming Emperor, Xiao Zhong, when a group of citizens attempted to seize the province of Tianzhou.

2. Hurry, shut the city gates and guard it with your dear lives.

Our soldiers have just left us. Who will guard it?

3. The newly appointed provincial governor, Kong Rong said:

We can only stop the attack for a few days. Perhaps the solution lies in showering the aggressors with our gifts and generosity.

4. I'm the governor, I'll go.

The aggressors are beyond reasoning. Who can talk to them?

Wisdom in
Quick-wittedness

1

A moment's change may lead to the start of a hundred-year-old plan.

Changes come like wind and fire, often too overpowering for the uninitiated.

3

The quick-minded will seize the opportunity to demonstrate their talents.

2

Walking speed varies from person to person. The differences may be negligible in short distances but not in long journeys.

4

5

It's like putting a bottle of good wine at the finishing line. Those who arrived first get drunk and those who come later could not even wet their lips.

6

So move the troops at lighting speed. Those who delay will be in the defensive.

Quick-mindedness is like the strong wind in Autumn, blowing the leaves off the trees speedily.

7

Reaction

灵变卷

Victory or defeat is decided in a day, even when a hundred battles are fought. War chariots which take three years to build can be destroyed in a single moment. The path to success is often filled with opportunities and changes.

The arrow trick

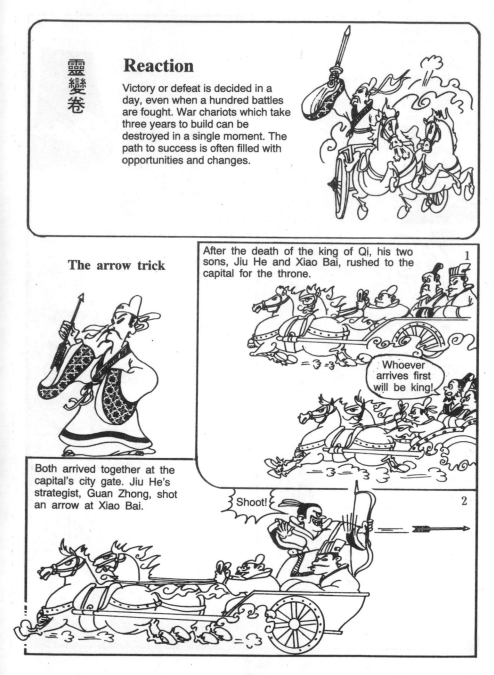

After the death of the king of Qi, his two sons, Jiu He and Xiao Bai, rushed to the capital for the throne.

1

Whoever arrives first will be king!

Both arrived together at the capital's city gate. Jiu He's strategist, Guan Zhong, shot an arrow at Xiao Bai.

Shoot!

2

Wisdom out of an emergency

1 Song Emperor, Wen Di, suffered heavy losses in weapons after a big defeat.

2 The head of the armoury, Gu Shen, discovered this:

The armoury is empty!

3 At a dinner, the emperor asked Gu Shen:

How much more weapons do we have?

There're too many people here to disclose such secrets. The emperor will be insulted if I didn't give an answer.

4 The emperor also realised he shouldn't have asked such a sensitive question.

5 We've enough arms for 100,000 troops and countless number of old weapons kept in secret.

Gu Shen's reply managed to save the emperor's face. At the same time he helped to keep the state's secrets intact.

Take advantage of the enemy's strength

1. The governor of the Weizhou, Cao Wei, was toasting with his army generals.

2. A few thousand men had revolted and defected to the enemy.

3. I ordered them to go.

4. This is a secret. Don't tell anyone.

5. On receiving the information, the enemy forces killed all the defectors.

This is a brilliant anti-espionage plan. It used the enemy's hand to discipline one's own rebellious troops.

Reflexes

應卒卷

Water far away cannot help put out a fire nearby. A simple meal before you is good enough to quench your thirst and fill your stomach. This is not to say we ignore what lies ahead. We must always remember to tackle the immediate problems first.

Finding the right antidote

1

After the Han ruler, Liu Bang, bestowed honours on over 20 of his officials, there were complaints from the others.

But I'm better qualified.

I've given more.

One day, Liu Bang met his advisor, Zhang Liang:

What are they quarrelling over?

2

104

The need for punishment

1 A fire broke out in the state of Lu, threatening the capital city.

The king led his men to put out the fire.

Where's everybody!

2

3 They're all after the animals running out from their hiding because of the fire.

4 The king sought Confucius' advice immediately.

What must I do?

105

106

Sensitivity

敏
悟
卷

A flower made from silk, however beautiful will be pale in comparison with the flowers of spring. This is because it lacks natural beauty. Those who are wise are naturally faster than the ordinary people in solving problems.

A child's politics

1. He's a bright kid.

Li Deyu was a gifted child. His father, Li Jipu, always praised him.

The Prime Minister, Wu Yuanheng, asked him:

What books do you read?

2. Li Deyu ran away without replying him.

4. Why were you so rude? Li Jipu was very angry after the incident.

As Prime Minister, he didn't ask me about politics but instead the books I read. My studies concern only school work and so I don't have to answer him.

Each department should only be concerned with affairs under its charge. There must not be confusion.

107

Relativity

Strength from nature's law

1 During the Song Dynasty, a bridge was suspended over a river with the help of eight iron-casted buffalos.

2 One day, a big flood destroyed the bridge and the buffalos sank to the bottom of the river. No one could bring them up.

Monk Huai Bing told the officials:

I can bring the iron buffalos up.

3

4 First, Huai Bing filled two boats with earth.

Wisdom in Strategy

The inch worm moves back so as to push itself forward.

5

6

These are methods and strategies!

9

The musk deer gives up its navel to ward off danger.

The birds of prey lie low in order to fly high.

The snake exposes its wound to frighten away any potential enemy.

7

8

10

Fools will not understand the strategies of the wise.

The wise can also make mistakes.

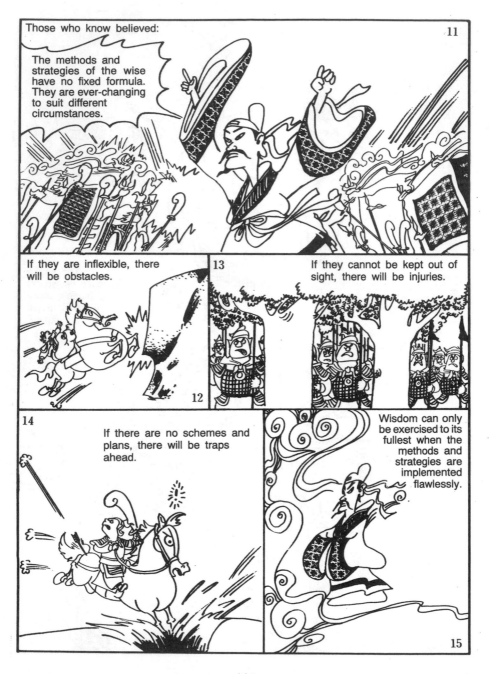

Crooked Thinking

委蛇卷

The ways with which the wise choose to solve life's problems are always impeccable. They are like the lotus flower, elegant and beautiful even though it came out of mud. Tackle all situations in different but clever sort of ways to avoid disasters and to achieve happiness.

Drunk together

1. King Zhou lost track of time after a night of drinking and merry making.
   What day is it?
   Don't know.

2. Ask Ji Zi.

3. The king asked you what day is it today?
   I'm drunk too and I can't remember.
   If the king, cannot lead with a clear mind, the country is in danger. If the others don't know and I know, I'm in trouble.

4. Be careful of your speech and actions at all times. It is better to exercise discretion than to be eager to show one's abilities.

Staying away from suspicion

1 Liu Bang's and Xiang Yu's troops were locked in battle outside the capital.

2 Liu Bang sent his special envoy to visit Xiao He in the capital many times.

The king sends his regards to you.

3 The king is away fighting and yet he sent his regards to you so many times. He is suspicious of you! For your own sake, please ask all your able brothers to join the army.

Bao Sheng told Xiao He:

I'll listen to you.

4 Liu Bang was very happy with what Xiao He had done.

Make Xiao He my Prime Minister. Send him a guard unit.

5 All the other officials congratulated Xiao He.

Congratulations!

Look after us.

Ha! Ha!

118

119

Nab the ring leader.

1. King Huan Gong of the state of Qi told Guan Zhong:

My officials are hoarding their wealth. They rather see their crops turned rotten than give them to the poor.

2. Guan Zhong said:

Punish the top official at Cheng Yang and the situation will change.

3. Why?

4. The official at Cheng Yang spent a lot of money for a life of luxury and pleasure.

5. But his brothers didn't even have enough to wear and eat.

6. Can he be loyal to the state?

A moral victory

1 The army of Qi attacked a hillock in the state of Zhao.

2 The Zhao general Kong Qing and his troops went to the rescue.

3 The Qi army was defeated and many of the troops were killed.

4 General Kong Qing gained a lot from the enemy's losses. He even built two huge graves to bury the 30,000 Qi soldiers who died in the battle.

權奇卷 Surprise

A threesome makes a tiger, so the saying goes. Never underestimate lies and falsehood. In military strategies there is no etiquette and one must be vigilant of the enemy's unreasonableness. Both the ways of the sincere and the dishonest are before you. Which way to follow depends on the effective results. One must never engage in empty talk like the scholars.

The false blinding the truth

1

The state of Jin captured Zheng Bo, the ruler of the state of Zheng.

Don't dream of returning!

2

If we asked Jin for our King, they'll surely refuse us!

Sun Shen, a senior Zheng official, said:

3

We should attack the state of Xu instead, to show Jin that we're prepared to have a new ruler.

After Zheng attacked Xu, the state of Jin re-examined the situation. Someone said:

The state of Zheng is not bothered by the capture of their ruler. I think they're ready for a new king.

If that is so, arresting Zheng Bo is no different from keeping any citizen.

Why don't we seek peace with Zheng through negotiations, using Zheng Bo's release as a condition?

Ha! Ha! I'm going home.

A peace agreement was reached between Jin and Zheng. Zheng Bo was released.

Use falsehood to camouflage the truth. Act cool when you're anxious. They are effective means to get what you want from your opponent.

Viewing the whole situation

1 Seven states, led by the states of Wu and Chu started a rebellion during the third year of Han Emperor, Xiao Jing's rule.

2 The king of Wu wants you to raise an army.

An envoy from Wu was sent to see King Huai Nan.

3 King Huai Nan consulted his Prime Minister:

Should I raise an army?

My king, if you agree to their request, I'm willing to lead the army.

The king wants you to send the troops out.

I only take orders from the Han Emperor.

6 King Huai Nan has lost his military power and so he didn't join the rebellion.

4 King Huai Nan gave his military power to the Prime Minister.

7 You are wrong . . . It's a mistake.

I sack you!

King Huai Nan was able to have protection in this way. But what if it was the work of a bookworm?

The means with which to achieve a goal isn't as important as sincerity.

The secret to fame

Wisdom in
Language

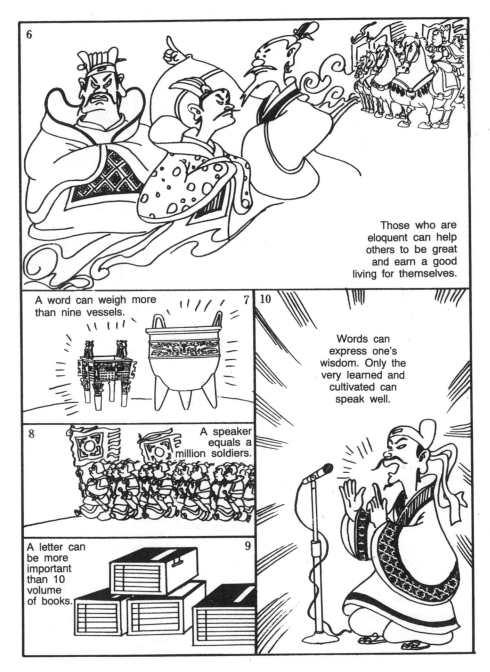

6

Those who are eloquent can help others to be great and earn a good living for themselves.

7

A word can weigh more than nine vessels.

10

Words can express one's wisdom. Only the very learned and cultivated can speak well.

8

A speaker equals a million soldiers.

9

A letter can be more important than 10 volume of books.

辩才卷

Argument

Official Gongzi Qiao was a pillar of the state of Zheng because of his eloquence. Lu Zhong sent a letter and helped the Qi army to destroy the city of Liao. There were many examples in history where highly intelligent officials used their eloquence to seek a solution in disputes at war.

Theory of a painful surrender

1 After their victory in a battle at Chang Ping, the state of Qin demanded six cities from Zhao, the loser.

2 To give or not to give?

The king of Zhao consulted Lou Huan who had returned from Qin.

3 For your sake, it's better to give what they want.

But Lu Qing disagreed.

They are tired.

4 Why is Qin's army withdrawing?

133

136

Eloquence

善言卷

Wisdom is behind the articulate, whose tongue is like that of a spring mechanism. The sage Mencius said: "You speak well using simple words to explain great truths." Well crafted and carefully planned speeches can help ward off danger with a laugh. Is there need to fight with weapons anymore?

Saved by speech

1 The emperor of Qin and Zhong Qi were quarrelling. No one was the winner.

2 I want you dead!

3 An official said: He's stubborn because his opponent is a wise and able king.

4 If he had met dictators like emperors Jie and Zhou, he would be dead long ago.

5 Right, I'll not blame him.

The mastery of speech can turn swords into ploughshares, and spears into pruning hooks.

Master of sarcasm

The emperor of Qi, Jin Gong's favourite horse was killed by the stable hand.

1

I'll kill you!

2

Don't let him die without knowing his crime.

Yan Zi stopped the emperor.

3

Let me spell out his offences one by one.

4

139

Wisdom in
Warfare

141

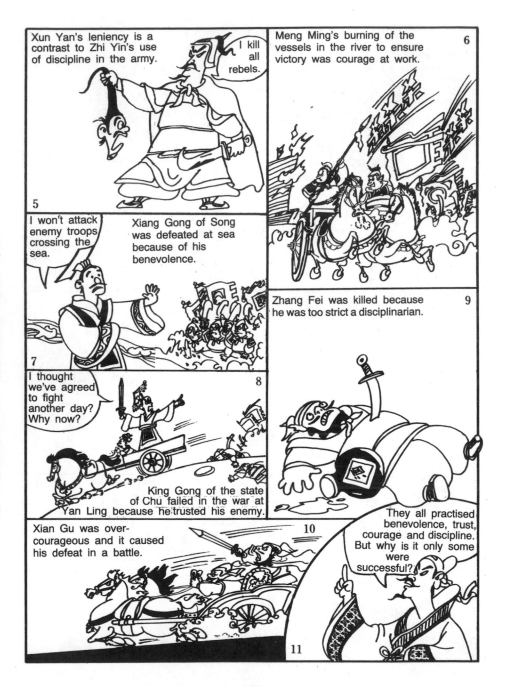

Yang Su sacrificed more than a thousand lives just to test the enemy. He won at the expense of benevolence. **12**

Zhao She cheated the Qin army by misplacing the trust given him in a counter espionage plan. **13**

16

They don't believe in benevolence, trust, discipline and courage. What's the secret of their success?

14 Li Guang was lenient towards his troops but was victorious despite the lack of discipline.

Han Xin suffered great humiliations and won without courage.

15

This is the difference between wisdom and folly. **17**

In a fight, the wiser will triumph. **18**

19

There are those who won without a fight and those who won a hundred battles. Some won in direct confrontations, others by using ingenuous plots or by springing a surprise. There were also those who won using age-old methods. But all used wisdom and strategies.

20

Yue Fei said:

Single-mindedness in execution is vital.

21

All schemes and plans.

A bookworm never knew the effectiveness of good military strategies.

22

To ensure peace and a good government, one cannot do without wisdom and strategies.

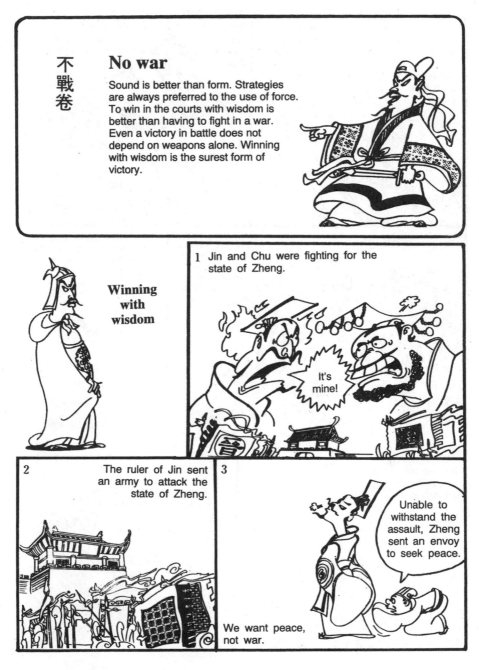

No war

不戰卷

Sound is better than form. Strategies are always preferred to the use of force. To win in the courts with wisdom is better than having to fight in a war. Even a victory in battle does not depend on weapons alone. Winning with wisdom is the surest form of victory.

Winning with wisdom

1 Jin and Chu were fighting for the state of Zheng.

It's mine!

2 The ruler of Jin sent an army to attack the state of Zheng.

We want peace, not war.

3 Unable to withstand the assault, Zheng sent an envoy to seek peace.

145

Exaggerating one's strength

1 It was the Spring and Autumn period when troops from Chu were attacking Zheng. Luan Shu led an army of Jin soldiers to the rescue. Both the armies met.

2 Xi Gong said:

3 The Chu army is underestimating the opponent and it can be easily shaken. If we create a false alarm by exaggerating our strength, we'll win in a night ambush.

Get our men to use more drums, beating them all at the same time to create noise.

4 In the night, the Jin's soldiers beat the drums.

Dong! Dong! Dong! Dong!

5 The Jin army defeated Chu's.

Dong! Dong!

Kill! Kill!

Exaggerating one's strength can frighten the enemy and at the same time raise the fighting spirit and morale of your troops. It's an effective strategy.

147

Don't act blindly.

149

151

制勝卷 Winning

There is no strategy which remains applicable forever because the condition of warfare changes all the time. The right approach is perhaps one which assesses the situation as a whole. Impatience may win over coldness, stillness over heat. The truly wise acts like the celestial dragon, which gets whatever it wants, winning in a hundred battles.

To win with patience

1 Han Zhong led 100,000 men to capture the city of Wan. Zhu Jun led another army to fight them back.

2 Zhu Jun was attacking from outside the city. Han Zhong was defending from inside the city, waving the white flag.

4 They were fighting hard with each other. But no one could win.

3 Accept their surrender and save the fighting.

No.

Create a false alarm to spring a surprise.

During the reign of Han Emperor, Guang Wu, Zhang Bu ordered his brother, Zhang Lan, to station 20,000 best soldiers to defend Xi An, an area in the present Shandong province. 1

Zhang Bu also relocated another 10,000 men from different counties to guard another city, Lin Zi which is only 40 miles from Xi An.

2 General Geng Mi of the Eastern Han Dynasty arrived between the two cities.

Xi An is small but tough to conquer.

Though bigger, Lin Zi is guarded by fewer men and an attack will be easier.

3

4 I've decided to attack Xi An in five days.

After five days, Geng Mi issued an order in the middle of night:

Eat now, attack Lin Zi.

5

Craftiness

詭道卷

We should be moderate in the conduct of our lives. But we need to be crafty in military strategy in order to create suspicion in the enemy. To be on the offensive and put the enemy forces in crisis, our minds must be clear. A flexible strategy capable of surprises will throw the enemy in disarray.

Unrestrained by old ways and methods

During the Eastern Han period, imperial guard Yu Xu was leading his men for a mission when he was stopped by soldiers of the Qiang tribal group.

2 Yu Xu spread rumours.

Yu Xu is waiting for reinforcement before advancing again.

The Qiang people stopped blocking Yu Xu's way. They went to the other countries and cities instead.

160

Winning by surprise

1. The armies of Wu and Yue were fighting at Zui Li. Gou Jian ordered: Form a death squad and charge!

2. The first charge failed. 刀槍不入！刀槍不入！

3. Again!

4. The second also failed. 刀槍不入！刀槍不入！

5. Their defence is too solid to go through.

6. Send prisoners on the death roll as the next group to the front line . . . Gou Jian said:

Yue's third death squad arrived before Wu's line of defence. 7

We are useless because we failed in our mission. We deserve to die! 8

After saying that, they slew themselves. 9

The men from the Wu's army were stunned. 10

Gou Jian seized the opportunity and won in a sudden attack. 11

To use prisoners as a disguise is a surprise.

163

Turn the enemy's strategy to one's advantage.

1 After his defeat, Huan Xuan moved to the west, leaving He Danzhi in the last line of defence. He Danzhi said:

Raise the flag in the vessel to disguise it as the commander's.

2 No point. He Danzhi is not in there.

Attack the vessel with the commander's flag.

He Wuji led an army in pursuit.

He Wuji said:

Since he is not there, the assault will be easy as the soldiers on board are not their best.

3 If we captured the vessel, the enemy would be thrown into chaos.

Oh no, the commander's vessel is under attack!

4

Records

武案卷

Doctors who follow closely to medical textbooks in their practice risk giving the wrong treatment. Generals who copy military strategies wholesale are likely to lose their armies. This is not to say it is useless to do studies, but that one must study well. The flags and banners of those before us serve as our guiding posts. Nature's beautiful mountains and rivers are the best learning materials for the artists.

It's good to be careful.

General Zong Ze of the Northern Song Dynasty plotted for the withdrawal of Jin soldiers from the state.

Ha! He's a fool! **1**

Zong Ze thought:

The Jin soldiers outnumbered us by 10 times, how can I force their withdrawal?

2

The Jin army will attack us tonight. Move our position quickly! **3**

But why?

The Jin's attack came but the Song troops were not there. **4**

It's good to be careful. Sometimes it's the little details which give hints to the calamities ahead.

The use of small things

The Southern Song general Liu Qi told his men in a battle at Shun Chang.

Take a bamboo container each and filled it with cooked beans.

The Song army threw the bamboo containers at the frontline before the battle.

3

The enemy's horses were hungry. They smelled the beans and bent their heads to search for the beans.

The bamboo containers were thrown everywhere. They distracted the horses and put the enemy forces in disarray. The Song army's offensive knocked them out completely.

Size is not important. Even the little things can yield big results when used well. Similarly, social class is not important. As long as the individual performs his best, they are capable of great contributions too.

4

The old horse knows best and lessons from the ant

Dividing and combining the forces

When the state of Yue attacked Wu, both their armies were stationed at opposite sides of the river.

1

2 3

The king of Yue ordered:

Divide the army into three!

In the evening, the king asked one group to move five miles upstream and another five miles downstream.

4

Dong! Dong!

Dong! Dong!

The same night, both groups beat their drums aloud.

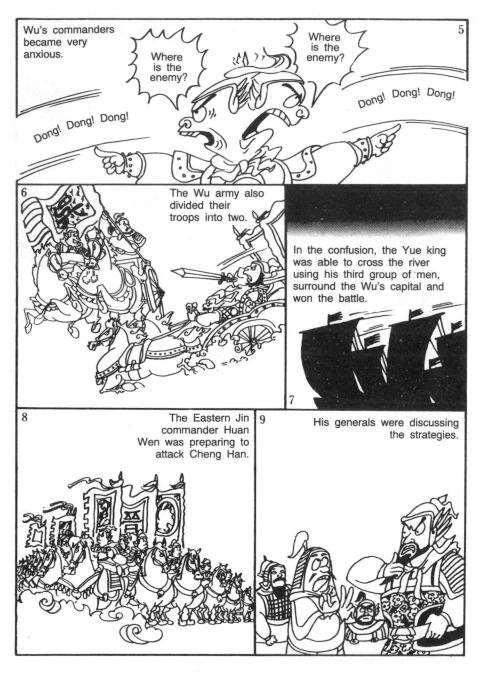

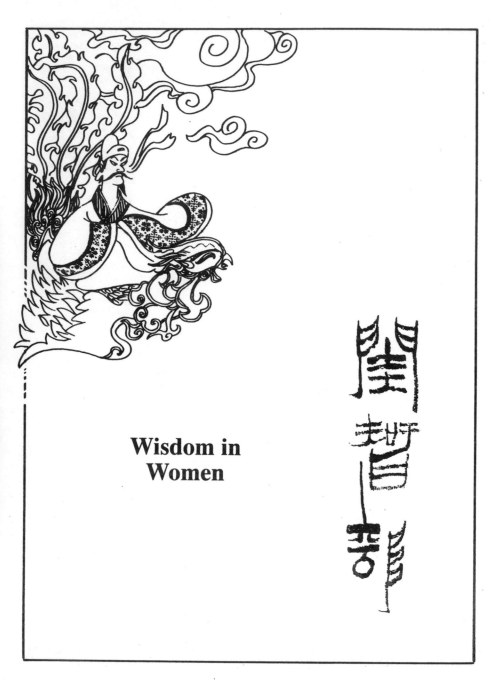

Wisdom in Women

175

6 Yi Jiang's talent was even praised by Confucius. But that didn't affect her impeccable character and virtues.

7 And is every stupid woman in the world virtuous?

8 If man represents the Sun, then woman represents the Moon.

The world needs the sunlight in the day as much as the moon's brightness at night.

Virtues

賢哲卷

There is stupidity because there is no talent. We can only learn from intelligence. There are many talents and wisdom hidden in women of the past. Men can learn from them too.

True understanding

The king of Qi sent an envoy to see Zhao's empress, Wei Hou.

1
Is the year's harvest good? Are the people well? Is the king healthy?

2
I'm sent here by the king and you didn't ask about his well-being first. You've your priorities all wrong.

3
I don't think so.

5 The cloth is made of silk. It is woven from an inch to a yard, from a yard to a bolt.

6 If you cut up the threads suddenly all efforts made will be lost. This is similar to abandoning one's studies halfway.

7 Yue Yangzi was very moved. He went away to study again, returning home only seven years later when he completed his studies.

8 While Yue Yangzi was away, his wife worked hard at home and looked after his mother.

9 Once, a neighbour's chicken ran into their house.

180

Choosing a general

1. The armies of Qin and Zhao were fighting at Chang Ping. The king of Zhao fell victim to Qin's counter espionage plan.

Lian Po is old and useless. Zhao Kuo, go replace him.

2. Zhao Kuo is not a good choice for general.

Zhao Kuo's mother told the king:

Why?

3. His father, Zhao She, had too many friends when he was a general.

Long live our friendship!

Forever friends.

4. And gave up all his rewards back to the military officers.

183

Knowing
oneself

184

185

Masculinity

雄略卷

Some men's behaviour resemble that of a shallow woman while there are women whose abilities match those of great men. Although they never step out of the house, they are able to think far ahead. We feel ashamed of our stupidity only when we discover their outstanding wisdom.

A brilliant diplomat

1. The Qin emperor sent a pair of locked jade rings to the empress in the state of Qi.

2. We heard the people of Qi are very intelligent. Can you unlock the rings?

3. Bang! Bang!

4. It's unlocked.

A bang and the jade rings broke into pieces. It upset Qin's plan to ridicule Qi.

Knowing others well

General Qu Xia of Chu was getting ready to capture the state of Luo. Dou Bobi sent him off.

Thank you.

I wish you luck.

1

2 Dou Bobi said after the send off:

He's too arrogant. He'll lose the battle.

3 Dou Bobi told the king:

Please send more troops to Qu Xia.

Where is there more army?

Why?

Dou Bobi is reminding you to punish Qu Xia with a threat.

The king's wife, Deng Man said: 4

Wisdom in Waywardness

6 This hand lotion was meant to prevent the skin of the naval forces from cracking.

This helped our army to win battles and I was promoted.

7 But others used it for a trivial reason.

You can wash one more piece of cloth with this lotion.

8 Those who know dirty tricks could also help Meng Changjun to escape ill luck.

Hey!

9 Thus, never give up any learning opportunity. If Mount Tai refused the small pieces of earth, it wouldn't be so high. If the ocean cut itself from the rivers and streams, it wouldn't be filled either.

10 I hope the sincere will learn something out of these and gain wisdom.

Wickedness

狡黠卷

Heroes have their strategies. But thugs also have their tricks. Intelligence and wisdom will develop with time but so will the devices of the cunning. Study their tricks thoroughly and one will not fall into their trap.

The theft of a country

1 The wife of the prince of Qin, Hua Yang, is childless. The prince's concubine, Xia Ji, however bore him a son, Yi Ren.

Sent him to Zhao as a hostage.

2 The state of Qin had attacked Zhao repeatedly. The life of Yi Ren was in danger.

You spy!

3 A businessman, Lü Buwei, met Yi Ren at Han Dan.

There's things to gain from him.

194

196

Paying lip-service

1 Someone told the king of Qi:

To prevent corruption in the court, you should hear reports of the accounts yourself.

True.

The Prime Minister, Tian Yin, said:

The reports are ready.

I'm ready.

2

Show all accounts, big or small, for the year together with supporting evidence.

Tian Yin instructed his officials:

3

The reports went on and on. **4**

Even past midnight, the reports were still coming. **5**

6 The king finally gave up.

You take care of it.

7 The ambitous Ming Dynasty official Liu Jin was greedy for power. He arranged many fun and games for the emperor.

8 When the emperor was enjoying himself, he brought stacks of documents for him to read and approve.

Please approve.

9 What are you good for? Why disturb me with all these matters?

After a few rounds, the emperor became angry.

10 Later, all matters, large or small, were under Liu Jin's control.

On the surface, they appear obedient. But inside, they're very vicious. There are far too many examples of such officials history.

201

Petty tricks

小慧卷

Rays coming through a small opening are from the sun. The tiny lights from a gathering of fire flies will bring brightness. The broadness of one's heart and mind can be compared with the ocean where water is both stored and received from the estuaries.

Weigh the pros and cons.

The king of Qi asked Su Dai: The king of Qin wants me to acknowledge him as emperor. What do you say?

1 If you don't agree, the king of Qin will be angry. But if you agree, the kings of the other states will be unhappy.

2 Why don't you agree with the king on the surface but take your time in accepting him as emperor formally. This will appease the rest.

3 If the rest of the world agreed with him after the king of Qin made himself emperor, then accept him. Otherwise, don't do it. Do one thing at a time.

All problems are different in nature. Weigh their relative importance and tackle them one at a time. The solutions will then become clearer to the mind.

203

A psychology test

During the period of the Five Dynasties, the king of Zhao, Li Decheng, from the Southern Tang Dynasty was in Jiangxi. A fortune teller told him:

I can tell the different classes of people with just one look.

Are you sure?

2 The king put his wife among a few court dancers, dressing her like them.

3 Sir, tell me who is my wife?

Give one some of his own medicine.

1. A medicine peddlar in Nanjing had a statue of Guanyin on his cart.

The goddess of mercy cures all.

2. He dropped his pills onto the goddess' hand.

3. Those which stucked onto the hand, he sold them to his customers.

4. Many came to see him for the medicine.

This is from the goddess of mercy.

5. Soon he became very rich.

6. A young man was very curious.

I'll find out the truth.

7. Can I buy you a drink?

A Brief Chronology of Chinese History

夏 Xia Dynasty			About 2100 – 1600 BC
商 Shang Dynasty			About 1600 – 1100 BC
周 Zhou Dynasty	西周 Western Zhou Dynasty		About 1100 – 771 BC
	東周 Eastern Zhou Dynasty		770 – 256 BC
	春秋 Spring and Autumn Period		770 – 476 BC
	戰國 Warring States		475 – 221 BC
秦 Qin Dynasty			221 – 207 BC
漢 Han Dynasty	西漢 Western Han		206 BC – AD 24
	東漢 Eastern Han		25 – 220
三國 Three Kingdoms	魏 Wei		220 – 265
	蜀漢 Shu Han		221 – 263
	吳 Wu		222 – 280
西晉 Western Jin Dynasty			265 – 316
東晉 Eastern Jin Dynasty			317 – 420
南北朝 Northern and Southern Dynasties	南朝 Southern Dynasties	宋 Song	420 – 479
		齊 Qi	479 – 502
		梁 Liang	502 – 557
		陳 Chen	557 – 589
	北朝 Northern Dynasties	北魏 Northern Wei	386 – 534
		東魏 Eastern Wei	534 – 550
		北齊 Northern Qi	550 – 577
		西魏 Western Wei	535 – 556
		北周 Northern Zhou	557 – 581
隋 Sui Dynasty			581 – 618
唐 Tang Dynasty			618 – 907
五代 Five Dynasties	後梁 Later Liang		907 – 923
	後唐 Later Tang		923 – 936
	後晉 Later Jin		936 – 946
	後漢 Later Han		947 – 950
	後周 Later Zhou		951 – 960
宋 Song Dynasty	北宋 Northern Song Dynasty		960 – 1127
	南宋 Southern Song Dynasty		1127 – 1279
遼 Liao Dynasty			916 – 1125
金 Jin Dynasty			1115 – 1234
元 Yuan Dynasty			1271 – 1368
明 Ming Dynasty			1368 – 1644
清 Qing Dynasty			1644 – 1911
中華民國 Republic of China			1912 – 1949
中華人民共和國 People's Republic of China			1949 –

Forthcoming...
(Strategy & Leadership)

WANG XUANMING

黃石公三略

HUANG SHIGONG'S STRATEGY

Translated by
Alan Chong
An Asiapac Publication

Forthcoming...
(*100 Series* Art Album)

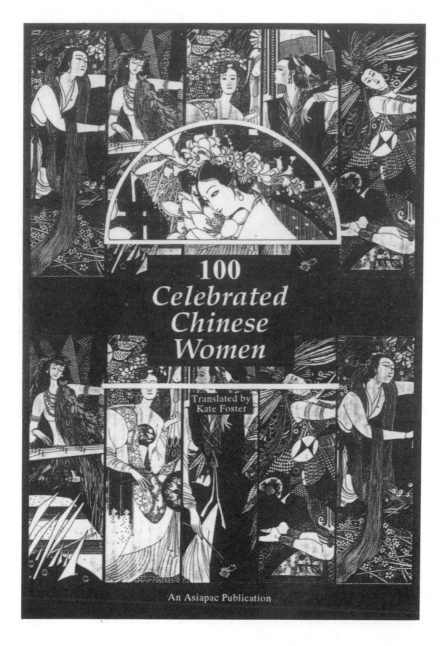

100
Celebrated
Chinese
Women

Translated by
Kate Foster

An Asiapac Publication

Asiapac Comic Series (by Tsai Chih Chung)

Art of War
Translated by Leong Weng Kam

The Art of War provides a compact set of principles essential for victory in battles; applicable to military strategists, in business and human relationships.

Book of Zen
Translated by Koh Kok Kiang

Zen makes the art of spontaneous living the prime concern of the human being. Tsai depicts Zen with unfettered versatility; his illustrations spans a period of more than 2,000 years.

Da Xue
Translated by Mary Ng En Tzu

The second book in the Four Books of the Confucian Classics. It sets forth the higher principles of moral science and advocates that the cultivation of the person be the first thing attended to in the process of the pacification of kingdoms.

Fantasies of the Six Dynasties
Translated by Jenny Lim

Tsai Chih Chung has creatively illustrated and annotated 19 bizarre tales of human encounters with supernatural beings which were compiled during the Six Dyansties (AD 220-589).

Lun Yu
Translated by Mary Ng En Tzu

A collection of the discourses of Confucius, his disciples and others on various topics. Several bits of choice sayings have been illustrated for readers in this book.

New Account of World Tales
Translated by Alan Chong

These 120 selected anecdotes tell the stories of emperors, princes, high officials, generals, courtiers, urbane monks and lettered gentry of a turbulent time. They afford a stark and amoral insight into human behaviour in its full spectrum of virtues and frailties and glimpses of brilliant Chinese witticisms, too.

Origins of Zen
Translated by Koh Kok Kiang

Tsai in this book traces the origins and development of Zen in China with a light-hearted touch which is very much in keeping with the Zen spirit of absolute freedom and unbounded creativity.

Records of the Historian
Translated by Tang Nguok Kiong

Adapted from Records of the Historian, one of the greatest historical work China has produced, Tsai has illustrated the life and characteristics of the Four Lords of the Warring Strates.

Roots of Wisdom
Translated by Koh Kok Kiang

One of the gems of Chinese literature, whose advocacy of a steadfast nature and a life of simplicity, goodness, quiet joy and harmony with one's fellow beings and the world at large has great relevance in an age of rapid changes.

Sayings of Confucius
Translated by Goh Beng Choo

This book features the life of Confucius, selected sayings from The Analects and some of his more prominent pupils. It captures the warm relationship between the sage and his disciples, and offers food for thought for the modern readers.

Sayings of Han Fei Zi
Translated by Alan Chong

Tsai Chih Chung retold and interpreted the basic ideas of legalism, a classical political philosophy that advocates a draconian legal code, embodying a system of liberal reward and heavy penalty as the basis of government, in his unique style.

Sayings of Lao Zi
Translated by Koh Kok Kiang & Wong Lit Khiong

The thoughts of Lao Zi, the founder of Taoism, are presented here in a light-hearted manner. It features the selected sayings from Dao De Jing.

Sayings of Lao Zi Book 2
Translated by Koh Kok Kiang

In the second book, Tsai Chih Chung has tackled some of the more abstruse passages from the Dao De Jing which he has not included in the first volume of Sayings of Lao Zi.

Sayings of Lie Zi
Translated by Koh Kok Kiang

A famous Taoist sage whose sayings deals with universal themes such as the joy of living, reconciliation with death, the limitations of human knowledge, the role of chance events.

Sayings of Mencius
Translated by Mary Ng En Tzu

This book contains stories about the life of Mencius and various excerpts from "Mencius", one of the Four Books of the Confucian Classics, which contains the philosophy of Mencius.

Sayings of Zhuang Zi
Translated by Goh Beng Choo

Zhuang Zi's non-conformist and often humorous views of life have been creatively illustrated and simply presented by Tsai Chih Chung in this book.

Sayings of Zhuang Zi Book 2
Translated by Koh Kok Kiang

Zhuang Zi's book is valued for both its philosophical insights and as a work of great literary merit. Tsai's second book on Zhuang Zi shows maturity in his unique style.

Strange Tales of Liaozhai
Translated by Tang Nguok Kiong

In this book, Tsai Chih Chung has creatively illustrated 12 stories from the Strange Tales of Liaozhai, an outstanding Chinese classic written by Pu Songling in the early Qing Dynasty.

Zhong Yong
Translated by Mary Ng En Tzu

Zhong Yong, written by Zi Si, the grandson of Confucius, gives voice to the heart of the discipline of Confucius. Tsai has presented it in a most readable manner for the modern readers to explore with great delight.

Other titles in Asiapac Comic Series

Thirty-six Stratagems
By Wang Xuanming
Translated by Koh Kok Kiang (cartoons) &
             Liu Yi (texts of the stratagems)
    A Chinese military classic which emphasizes deceptive schemes to achieve military objectives. It has attracted the attention of military authorities and general readers alike.

Curry Puff
By Raymond Lee
    A collection of tidbit-sized pieces of humour with a distinct Singaporean flavour, intended to act as one-shot stings of excitement. Its title comes from the protagonist's hairdo which resembles Singapore's favourite snack – curry puff.

Dream Allegory
By Wee Tian Beng
Translated by Jenny Lim
    A local cartoonist who has spun his yarns – Dream Allegory and Dream Fantasy – creatively in the scenes of Singapore. Hence making it uniquely Singaporean.

Jim's Corner – Life in the 60s
By Jim Yong
    Jim has enlivened the lives of the Singaporeans in the 1960s in this book, capturing the scenes of the former days through his personal encounters, adding lots of humour and jests.

Who's the Boss?!
By Tan Wee Lian
    This book of witty and entertaining comics gives you a peep into what's life after marriage in the 1990s – from children and in-laws to neighbours and their gossips!

Hilarious Chinese Classics by Tsai Chih Chung

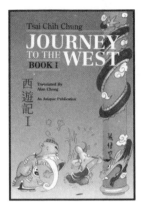

Journey to the West 1

These books offer more than the all-too-familiar escapades of Tan Sanzang and his animal disciples. Under the creative pen of Tsai Chih Chung, *Journey to the West* still stays its course but takes a new route. En route from ancient China to India to acquire Buddhist scriptures, the Monk and his disciples veer off course frequently to dart into modern times to have fleeting exchanges with characters ranging from Ronald Reagan to Bunny Girls of the Playboy Club.

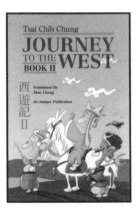

Journey to the West 2

Romance of the Three Kingdoms

Set in the turbulent Three Kingdoms Period, *Romance of the Three Kingdoms* relates the clever political manoeuvres and brilliant battle strategies used by the ambitious rulers as they fought one another for supremacy.

In this comic version, Tsai Chih Chung has illustrated in an entertaining way the four best-known episodes in the novel. Don't be surprised to see a warrior waving an Iraqi flag, a satellite dish fixed on top of an ancient Chinese building, and court officials playing mahjong or eating beef noodles, a favourite Taiwanese snack.

《亞太漫畫系列》

智謀叢畫

智囊

編著：王宣銘

翻譯：梁榮錦

亞太圖書有限公司出版

Contents